THE SONGS FROM THE MUSICAL BY

ANDREW LLOYD WEBBER

BASED ON 'OLD POSSUM'S BOOK OF PRACTICAL CATS' BY

T. S. ELIOT

FABER MUSIC LTD
3 QUEEN SQUARE   LONDON WC1

THE REALLY USEFUL GROUP plc

Distributed by

HAL LEONARD PUBLISHING CORPORATION

Winona, MN 55987   Milwaukee, WI 53213

Cats is recorded on Geffen Records/Warner Bros. Records

CONTENTS

I began setting *Old Possum's Book of Practical Cats* to music late in 1977, partly because it is a book I remember with affection from my childhood and partly because I wanted to set existing verse to music. When I have written with lyricists in the past we have agreed together the dramatic structure, but for the most part the lyrics have been written to the music. So I was intrigued to see whether I could write a complete piece the other way round.

Very luckily *Old Possum* contains verses that are extraordinarily musical; they have rhythms that are very much their own, like the 'Rum Tum Tugger' or 'Old Deuteronomy' and, although clearly they dictate to some degree the music that will accompany them, they are frequently of irregular and exciting metre and are very challenging to a composer.

My first plans were for a concert anthology, and it was with this in mind that some of my settings were performed in the summer of 1980 at the Sydmonton Festival. Mrs Eliot fortunately came to the concert and brought with her various unpublished pieces of verse by her husband, including 'Grizabella: the Glamour Cat.' The musical and dramatic images that this created for me made me feel that there was very much more to the project than I had realized. In Trevor Nunn I found a collaborator with a taste for tackling theatrical problems that most people would consider insoluble. Together we worked out a dramatic structure for a full evening, helped by further unpublished Eliot material that Mrs Eliot kindly provided and by the many references to cats in the the main body of his writing. The show, as its form emerged, gave me an exciting opportunity to compose dance music and I was fortunate to be guided through the unfamiliar world of choreography by someone as experienced as Gillian Lynne.

I enjoyed working on *Cats* as much as on any show on which I have worked. My gratitude will be undying to Valerie Eliot without whose encouragement it could never have taken its present form.

Cats opened at the New London Theatre on May 11th 1981. This folio contains most of the music from the London production as recorded on the Polydor double record album. For reasons of space there are inevitably some omissions, principally the longer dance sections and the extended setting of 'The Pekes and the Pollicles'. There are also some small alterations and cuts, notably in the Prologue 'Jellicle Songs for Jellicle Cats'.

T. S. Eliot wrote the *Old Possum* poems in a series of letters to his godchildren and it is almost certain that their parents were just as much the intended recipients of the poems as those children. I hope that the music of *Cats* achieves the sense of fun that abounds in Eliot's verse.

ANDREW LLOYD WEBBER

A Note on the Text

Most of the poems comprising *Old Possum's Book of Practical Cats* (1939) have been set to music complete and in their originally published form; a few have been subject to a minor revision of tense or pronoun, and eight lines have been added to 'The Song of the Jellicles'. However, some of our lyrics, notably 'The Marching Song of the Pollicle Dogs' and the story of 'Grizabella', were discovered among the unpublished writings of Eliot. The prologue is based on ideas and incorporates lines from another unpublished poem, entitled 'Pollicle Dogs and Jellicle Cats'. 'Memory' includes lines from and is suggested by 'Rhapsody on a Windy Night', and other poems of the Prufrock period. All other words in the show are taken from the Collected Poems.

TREVOR NUNN

Overture

Music by
ANDREW LLOYD WEBBER

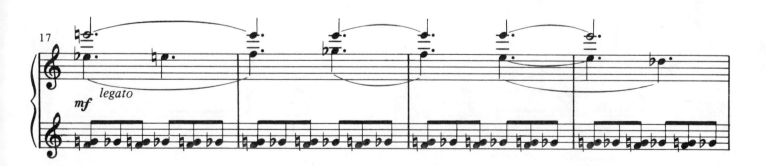

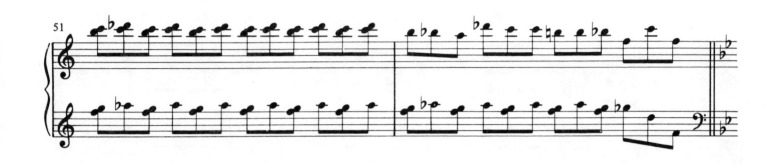

Jellicle Songs for Jellicle Cats

Music by
ANDREW LLOYD WEBBER

Text by
TREVOR NUNN and RICHARD STILGOE
after T.S. ELIOT

Attacca 'The Naming of Cats'

The Naming of Cats

Music by
ANDREW LLOYD WEBBER

Text by
T.S. ELIOT

CHORUS *(spoken in rhythm)*

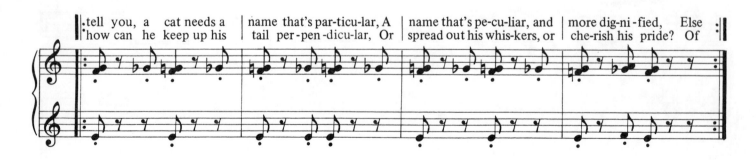

thought of his |name: His in -|eff-a-ble |eff-a-ble |Eff - an - in -

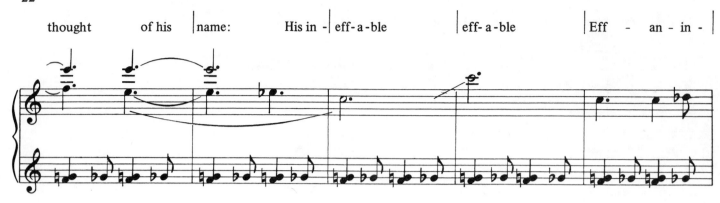

- ef-fa-ble |Deep and in-|scru-ta-ble |sin-gu-lar |name.

repeat to fade

The Invitation to the Jellicle Ball

Jellicle Cats come out tonight,
Jellicle Cats come one come all:
The Jellicle Moon is shining bright —
Jellicles come to the Jellicle Ball.

Jellicle Cats meet once a year
At the Jellicle Ball where we all rejoice,
And the Jellicle leader will soon appear
And make what is known as the Jellicle choice —

When Old Deuteronomy just before dawn,
Through a silence you feel you can cut with a knife,
Announces the cat who can now be reborn
And come back to a different Jellicle life.

For waiting up there is the Heavyside Layer,
Full of wonders one Jellicle only will see,
And Jellicles ask, because Jellicles dare:
Who will it be? Who will it be?

The Old Gumbie Cat

Music by
ANDREW LLOYD WEBBER

Text by
T.S. ELIOT

sits and sits and sits and sits, ___ and that's what makes a Gum - bie

Am7 Am6 Em7 Fmaj7 Bb7 B7

rall.

CHORUS

Cat, that's what makes_ a ___ Gum - bie ___ Cat! But

C7 Am7 Bm7 B7 Em

Sprightly [♩ = 104]

when the day's hus - tle and bus - tle is done,_ Then the Gum-bie Cat's work_ is but

Sprightly [♩ = 104]

sim. stacc.

Cm B(b5) Eb/Bb A° Ab7 G7

hard - ly be - gun._ { As she finds that the mice will not e - ver keep quiet,_ She is
She thinks that the cock - roa - ches just need em - ploy - ment To pre-

Cm Cm6 G7 Cm B(b5) Eb/Bb A°

tucks up her skirts____ to the base-ment to creep. She is deep-ly con-cerned____ with the
sure it is due____ to ir - reg - u -lar diet____ And be-
vent them from i - dle and wan - ton des -troy - ment. So she's

A♭7   G7   Cm   A♭

ways of the mice:____ Their be - ha-viour's not good____ and their man-ners not nice;____ So

B♭   B♭7   E♭   E♭maj7   A♭maj7

when she has got____them lined up____ on the mat - ting,____ She tea-ches them mu - sic, cro-chet-

D♭   D♭   G7

SOLO

- ting and tat - ting. I -liev- ing that no - thing is done____ with-out try - ing, She sets

Cm   A♭   B♭   B♭7

ev - en cre - a - ted a Bee - tles' Tat - too. ___

The Rum Tum Tugger

Music by
ANDREW LLOYD WEBBER

Text by
T.S. ELIOT

CHORUS
on-ly want a rat, If you set me on a rat then I'd ra-ther chase a mouse. The
bur - eau drawer, But I make such a fuss if I can't get out. The
E7
Dm7/G
Dm7/G
R.T. TUGGER
Rum Tum Tug - ger is a Cur - i - ous Cat, And there is-n't an-y call for me to shout it:
Rum Tum Tug - ger is a Cur - i - ous Cat, And it is-n't an-y use for you to doubt it:
A♯9
CHORUS
R.T. TUGGER
For he will do as he do do And there's no do-ing a-ny-thing a - bout it!
1
D
A/E
F♯m
A/E
CHORUS
The

Bustopher Jones: the Cat about Town

Music by
ANDREW LLOYD WEBBER

Text by
T.S. ELIOT

Bus-to-pher Jones____ is not skin and bones,____ In fact he's re-mar-ka-bly fat.____
cat we all greet___ as he walks down the street___ In his coat of fas-ti - di-ous black:___

He does-n't haunt pubs,___ he has eight or nine clubs,___ For
No com-mon place mou-sers___ have such well-cut trou-sers___ Or

he's the St. Jame-s's Street Cat!___ He's the   such an im-pec-ca-ble back.___

In the whole of St. Jame-s's the smart-est of names__ is The name of this Brum-mell__ of cats;__ And we're all of us proud__ to be nod-ded or bowed__ to By Bus - to - pher Jones in white spats!__

Slower [♩ = 92]

BUSTOPHER JONES

My vi-sits are oc-ca-sion-al to the *Se-nior E - du - ca-tion-al* And

season of ven-'son I give my ben-'son to the Pot-hun-ter's suc-cu-lent bones; And

just be-fore noon's not a mo-ment too soon To drop in for a drink at the

Drones._____ When I'm seen in a hur-ry there's pro-ba-bly cur-ry At the

Si-am-ese or at the Glut-ton;__ If I look full of gloom then I've

(funereal)

Mungojerrie and Rumpelteazer

Music by
ANDREW LLOYD WEBBER

Text by
T.S. ELIOT

Mun - go - jer - rie and Rum - pel - tea - zer were a no - tor - i - ous
Mun - go - jer - rie and Rum - pel - tea - zer had an un - u - su - al

coup - le of cats._ As knock - a - bout clowns, quick change com - e - di - ans,
gift of the gab._ They were high - ly ef - fi - cient cat bur - glars as well and re -

tight rope walk - ers and ac - ro - bats._ They had an ex - ten - sive
mark - a - bly smart at a smash and grab. They made their home in Vic -

44

won-der-ful way of work-ing to-geth- er.__ And some of the time you would

say it was luck, and some of the time_ you would say____ it was weath-er.__ They'd

go through the house like a hur-ri-cane, and no so-ber per-son could

Ab

take__ his oath__ Was it Mun-go-jer-rie or Rum-pel-tea-zer? or

could you have sworn that it might-n't be both? And when you heard a

Bb7(#5)   Bb13   Eb   F

din-ing-room smash Or up from the pan-try there came a loud crash_ Or

down from the lib-ra-ry came a loud ping From a vase which was com-mon-ly

(b)Db

said to be Ming; Then the fam-i-ly would say: "Now

Bb7(#5)

Old Deuteronomy

Music by
ANDREW LLOYD WEBBER

Text by
T.S. ELIOT

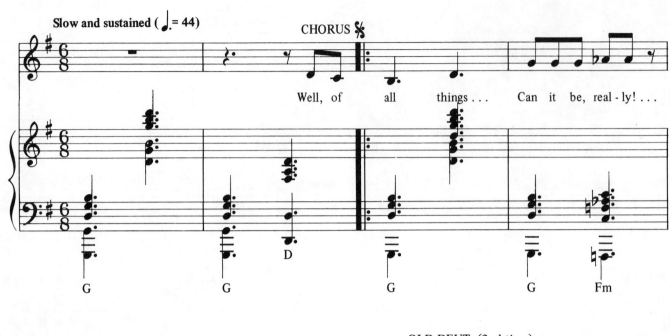

The Awefull Battle of the Pekes and the Pollicles

OF THE AWEFULL BATTLE
OF THE PEKES AND THE POLLICLES
Together with some Account
of the Participation
of the Pugs and the Poms, and
the Intervention of the Great Rumpuscat

The Pekes and the Pollicles, everyone knows,
Are proud and implacable passionate foes;
It is always the same, wherever one goes.
And the Pugs and the Poms, although most people say
That they do not like fighting, yet once in a way,
They will now and again join in to the fray
And they
      Bark bark bark bark
      Bark bark BARK BARK
Until you can hear them all over the Park.

Now on the occasion of which I shall speak
Almost nothing had happened for nearly a week
(And that's a long time for a Pol or a Peke).
The big Police Dog was away from his beat —
I don't know the reason, but most people think
He'd slipped into the Wellington Arms for a drink —
And no one at all was about on the street
When a Peke and a Pollicle happened to meet.
They did not advance, or exactly retreat,
But they glared at each other, and scraped their hind feet,
And started to
      Bark bark bark bark
      Bark bark BARK BARK
Until you could hear them all over the Park.

Now the Peke, although people may say what they please,
Is no British Dog, but a Heathen Chinese.
And so all the Pekes, when they heard the uproar,
Some came to the window, some came to the door;
There were surely a dozen, more likely a score.
And together they started to grumble and wheeze
In their huffery-snuffery Heathen Chinese.
But a terrible din is what Pollicles like,
For your Pollicle Dog is a dour Yorkshire tyke.

There are dogs out of every nation,
The Irish, the Welsh and the Dane;
The Russian, the Dutch, the Dalmatian,
And even from China and Spain;
The Poodle, the Pom, the Alsatian
And the mastiff who walks on a chain.
And to those that are frisky and frollical
Let my meaning be perfectly plain:
That my name it is Little Tom Pollicle —
And you'd better not do it again.

And his braw Scottish cousins are snappers and biters,
And every dog-jack of them notable fighters;
And so they stepped out, with their pipers in order,
Playing *When the Blue Bonnets Came Over the Border*.
Then the Pugs and the Poms held no longer aloof,
But some from the balcony, some from the roof,
Joined in
To the din
With a
      Bark bark bark bark
      Bark bark BARK BARK
Until you could hear them all over the Park.

Now when these bold heroes together assembled,
The traffic all stopped, and the Underground trembled,
And some of the neighbours were so much afraid
That they started to ring up the Fire Brigade.
When suddenly, up from a small basement flat,
Why who should stalk out but the GREAT RUMPUSCAT.
His eyes were like fireballs fearfully blazing,
He gave a great yawn, and his jaws were amazing;
And when he looked out through the bars of the area,
You never saw anything fiercer or hairier.
And what with the glare of his eyes and his yawning,
The Pekes and the Pollicles quickly took warning.
He looked at the sky and he gave a great leap —
And they every last one of them scattered like sheep.

And when the Police Dog returned to his beat,
There wasn't a single one left in the street.

The Song of the Jellicles

Music by
ANDREW LLOYD WEBBER

Text by
T.S. ELIOT

CHORUS *(spoken in rhythm)*

Jel - li - cle Cats come | out to - night, | Jel - li - cle Cats come | one come all: The
Jel - li - cle Moon is | shin - ing bright: | Jel - li - cles come to the | Jel - li - cle Ball.

Jel - li - cle Cats are | black and white, | Jel - li - cle Cats are | ra - ther small;
Jel - li - cle Cats are | mer - ry and bright, And | plea - sant to hear when we | cat - er - waul.

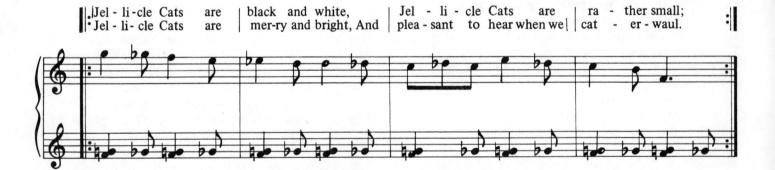

Jel - li - cle Cats have | cheer - ful fa - ces, | Jel - li - cle Cats have | bright black eyes; We
like to prac - tise our | airs and graces, And | wait for the Jel - li - cle | Moon to rise.

Jel - li - cle Cats de - | ve - lop slow-ly, | Jel - li - cle Cats are | not too big;
Jel - li - cle Cats are | ro - ly po-ly We | know how to dance a ga - | votte and a jig. Un -

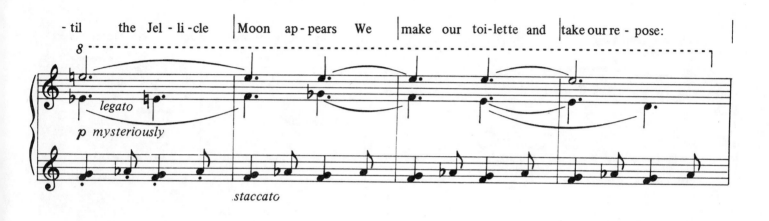

- til the Jel - li - cle | Moon ap - pears We | make our toi-lette and | take our re - pose:

Jel - li - cles wash be - | hind their ears, | Jel - li - cles dry be - | tween their toes.

Jel - li - cle Cats are | white and black, | Jel - li - cle Cats are of | mod-e-rate size;
Jel - li - cles jump like a | jump-ing jack, | Jel - li - cle Cats have | moon-lit eyes. We're

quiet e - nough in the | mor - ning hours, We're | quiet e - nough in the | af - ter - noon, Re -

- ser - ving our terp - si - | chor - e - an powers To | dance by the light of the | Jel - li - cle Moon.

mysteriously

Jel - li - cle Cats are | black and white, | Jel - li - cle Cats (as we | said) are small; If it

hap - pens to be a | stor - my night We will | prac - tise a ca - per or | two in the hall. If it

Here follows 'The Jellicle Ball'.

Grizabella: the Glamour Cat

Music by
ANDREW LLOYD WEBBER

Text by
T.S. ELIOT

Was Gri - za - bel - la, the Gla - mour Cat!

Ebm   Bbm/F   Em   Abm

The Moments of Happiness

The moments of happiness . . .
We had the experience but missed the meaning,
And approach to the meaning restores the experience
In a different form, beyond any meaning
We can assign to happiness . . .
. . . the past experience revived in the meaning
Is not the experience of one life only
But of many generations — not forgetting
Something that is probably quite ineffable . . .

(from T.S. Eliot 'The Dry Salvages' in *Four Quartets*)

Gus: the Theatre Cat

Music by
ANDREW LLOYD WEBBER

Text by
T.S. ELIOT

act-ed with Irv-ing, he's act-ed with Tree. And he
Gal-le-ry once gave him sev-en cat- calls. But his

G   D/F#   F#7   Bm   Bm

grand-est cre-a-tion, as he loves to tell, Was Fire-frore-fid-dle, the

G F#m7 Em9 G/A   Bm   Bm   Em7 F#m7 Gmaj7 G/A

Dal Segno

GUS

Fiend of the Fell.   I have

Csus2   G   D

CODA

cat. But my grand-est cre-a-tion, as his-tory will tell, Was

Bm   G F#m7 Em9   G/A   Bm   Bm

GUS (Sung reprise)

And I once crossed the stage on a telegraph wire,
To rescue a child when a house was on fire.
And I think that I still can much better than most,
Produce blood-curdling noises to bring on the Ghost.
I once played Growltiger, could do it again . . .

attacca 'Growltiger's Last Stand'

Growltiger's Last Stand

Music by
ANDREW LLOYD WEBBER
[♩ = 116]

Text by
T.S. ELIOT

CHORUS

Growl-tig-er was a Bra-vo Cat, who tra-velled on a barge: In fact he was the rough-est cat that ev-er roamed at large. From Graves-end up to Ox-ford he pur-sued his e-vil aims, Re--joi-cing in his ti-tle of 'The Ter-ror of the Thames'. His

sam-pans cir-cled round, And yet from all the e - ne - my there was not heard a sound. The

foe was armed with toast-ing forks and cru-el carv-ing knives, And the lov-ers sang their last du-et, in dan-ger of their lives.

rall.

a tempo Presto [♩ = 140]

Then Gilbert gave the signal to
his fierce Mongolian horde;

With a frightful burst of fireworks the

Chinks they swarmed aboard.

ff a tempo

Presto [♩ = 140]

Then Grid - dle - bone she

*Here follows 'The Ballad of Billy M'Caw' (p. 74)

The Ballad of Billy M'Caw

Music by
ANDREW LLOYD WEBBER

Text by
T.S. ELIOT

SOLO [GROWLTIGER]

Oh, how well I re-mem-ber the old Bull and Bush, Where we used to go down of a Sat-ta-day night, Where, when a-ny-think hap-pened, it come with a rush, For the boss, Mr Clark, he was ve-ry po-lite; A ve-ry nice House, from base-ment to gar-ret A ve-ry nice House. Ah, but it was the par-ret, The

78

Skimbleshanks: the Railway Cat

Music by
ANDREW LLOYD WEBBER

Text by
T. S. ELIOT

SKIMBLE
(2nd time)

Macavity: the Mystery Cat

Music by
ANDREW LLOYD WEBBER

Text by
T.S. ELIOT

-a-vi-ty's_ not there! You may seek him in the base-ment, you may look up in the air:

But I tell you once and once a-gain, Mac-a-vi-ty's_ not there! Mac-

G7

-a-vi-ty's a gin-ger cat, he's ve-ry tall and thin;_ You would know him if you saw him, for his

Cm   Cm/E♭   F   G7   Cm   Cm/E♭

eyes are sun-ken in. __ His brow is deep-ly lined with thought, his head is high-ly domed; His

F   G7

Mr. Mistoffelees

Music by
ANDREW LLOYD WEBBER

Text by
T.S. ELIOT

SOLO You ought to ask Mr. Mistoffelees!
The Original Conjuring Cat.
The great-est ma - gi - cians have some-thing to learn_ From

Mis - ter Mis - tof - fel - ee - s's Con - jur - ing Turn._ Pre - sto! And we all say:

CHORUS
Oh! Well I ne - ver! Was_there e - ver a cat so cle-ver as Ma - gi - cal Mis - ter Mis - tof -

- fel -ees!   - fel -ees!

SOLO
He is   quiet, he is small, he is black   From his
His   manner is   vague and a-loof,   You would

Memory

Music by
ANDREW LLOYD WEBBER

Text by
TREVOR NUNN
after T.S. ELIOT

[Grizabella is chosen to go to the Heavyside Layer.]

(alternate lyric)

MEMORY

Text by TREVOR NUNN
after T.S. ELIOT

DAYLIGHT, SEE THE DEW ON A SUNFLOWER
AND A ROSE THAT IS FADING
ROSES WITHER AWAY
LIKE THE SUNFLOWER I YEARN TO TURN MY FACE TO THE DAWN
I AM WAITING FOR THE DAY

MEMORY, TURN YOUR FACE TO THE MOONLIGHT
LET YOUR MEMORY LEAD YOU
OPEN UP, ENTER IN
IF YOU FIND THERE THE MEANING OF WHAT HAPPINESS IS
THEN A NEW LIFE WILL BEGIN

MEMORY, ALL ALONE IN THE MOONLIGHT
I CAN SMILE AT THE OLD DAYS
I WAS BEAUTIFUL THEN
I REMEMBER THE TIME I KNEW WHAT HAPPINESS WAS
LET THE MEMORY LIVE AGAIN

BURNT OUT ENDS OF SMOKEY DAYS
THE STALE COLD SMELL OF MORNING
THE STREELAMP DIES, ANOTHER NIGHT IS OVER
ANOTHER DAY IS DAWNING

DAYLIGHT, I MUST WAIT FOR THE SUNRISE
I MUST THINK OF A NEW LIFE
AND I MUSTN'T GIVE IN
WHEN THE DAWN COMES TONIGHT WILL BE A MEMORY TOO
AND A NEW DAY WILL BEGIN

SUNLIGHT, THROUGH THE TREES IN SUMMER
ENDLESS MASQUERADING
LIKE A FLOWER AS THE DAWN IS BREAKING
THE MEMORY IS FADING

TOUCH ME, IT'S SO EASY TO LEAVE ME
ALL ALONE WITH THE MEMORY
OF MY DAYS IN THE SUN
IF YOU TOUCH ME YOU'LL UNDERSTAND WHAT HAPPINESS IS
LOOK, A NEW DAY HAS BEGUN

The Journey to the Heavyside Layer

Music by
ANDREW LLOYD WEBBER

Text by
T. S. ELIOT

* For complete instrumental, take in bars 61 to 88 of Overture (pp. 8–10)

The Ad-dressing of Cats

Music by
ANDREW LLOYD WEBBER

Text by
T.S. ELIOT

learnt a-bout our pro-per names, Our ha-bits and our ha-bi-tat: But
fre-quent-ly un-dig-ni-fied. He's such an ea-sy-go-ing lout, He'll

Bb/F   Gm   Bb/F   Gm

CHORUS

How would you ad-dress a cat? *f* So
an-swer a-ny hail or shout. The

Bb/F   Eb/F   Bb   Eb/Bb

first, your me-mo-ry I'll jog, And say: a cat is not a
us-ual dog a-

Bb   Eb/Bb   Bb   Gm   Bb/F   Eb Bb/D Cm Bb   F   Eb

OLD DEUTERONOMY

dog.   *mp* Now

Bb   F/Bb   Eb/Bb   F7/Bb (no 5th)